CONTENTS

GW00691423

Welcome

I'm really excited to be able to guide you through each stage of our RYA Youth Windsurfing Scheme, from your first steps on a board to placing your feet in the straps for the first time.

Amanda Van Santen
RYA Chief Instructor, Dinghy & Windsurfing

RYA
Youth **Windsurfing**
SCHEME

Without the RYA Windsurfing Scheme, all three of us would undoubtedly not be where we are today. From the very beginning there was a clear route of how to progress if you wanted to, following a route in windsurfing that was recreational, racing or both.

The Team15 initiative was the start for all of us. We all have great memories of fun, low-key racing where we competed for our home club and chose to progress along our racing pathway.

From Team15, we went into an RYA Zone Squad. We all had a great time being members of the Zone Squad, which gave us a platform for a natural step up into the RYA National Junior Squad. Training with the National Junior Squad was always really fun!

We are all now proud members of the British Sailing Team and look back with very fond memories of the RYA's pathway, including our first times representing GBR, really enjoyable training camps during the winter months and travelling the country and the world making lifelong friends!

Imogen Sills
Sam Sills
Saskia Sills

Introduction

The RYA Youth Windsurfing Scheme provides you with an easy and accessible way to progress in this exciting sport, with a certificated course for you to log your progression and recognise your achievements.

RYA YOUTH TRAINING SYLLABUS

The RYA Youth Windsurfing Scheme has been designed to relate directly to the adult syllabus in the RYA National Windsurfing Scheme, providing ease of use and comparison.

Youth Stage 2 is equivalent to Start Windsurfing and Youth Stage 4 to Intermediate Windsurfing in the RYA National Windsurfing Scheme. Once you have completed Youth Stage 4, why stop there? You have all the skills and ability to further your progression through the Advanced Windsurfing course and specific clinics.

If you see *'Knowledge of'*, generally it means your instructor will talk through some information and then guide you as to where to find out more.

Where you see *'Understands'*, your instructor will cover the subject in depth and may ask you to demonstrate, with assistance if necessary.

As you progress through the scheme, your instructor will cover activities, such as tacking and gybing, and make sure you *Can* perform them before they sign your certificate off.

Use the wallchart and stickers to see how well you're doing!

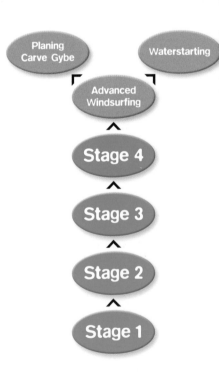

'TAKE THE CHALLENGE AND LOG YOUR RESULTS'

These are not part of the main certificates, just fun things for you to try to get your instructor to sign off. Featuring a mixture of racing and freestyle challenges, you will improve your skills and techniques dramatically in all aspects of windsurfing by just being out on the water on a board and a rig.

Freestyle and racing, and all the skills and moves that are required (and those that are yet to be discovered!) relate to all aspects of windsurfing – from competition to cruising, and from flat-water inland locations to coastal wavy ones.

One of the best things about windsurfing is that it has no age or ability restrictions – it's open to everyone.

Look out for this symbol throughout the book!

Fancy a go at Racing?

The RYA Youth Racing Syllabus has three levels: Start, Intermediate and Advanced. Having completed Youth Stage 1 windsurfing, you'll be at the right level to begin the Start Racing course. As you get better, you can progress until you have done your Advanced level, by which time you will be giving the world's best a run for their money!

Advanced Racing

∧

Intermediate Racing

∧

Start Racing

With a network of Team15 clubs and local events to help introduce you to the fun of racing, you may want to take a step further and progress to achieve your true potential. For further information on racing and Team15 please see page 40.

TRAINING SYLLABUS

YOUTH
Stage 1

This is an ideal first introduction with no prior experience needed. Youth Stage 1 will teach you the basics of getting on the water and sailing the board across the wind and back.

PRACTICAL

Launching, Starting and Landing

Can:

- GC • Put on a wetsuit and buoyancy aid
- GC • Stand the rig up on land:
- GC   - Lean the rig slowly from side to side
- GC   - Balance the rig and clap your hands
- GC   - Use the wind to fill and empty the sail

Has practical understanding of *(with assistance if required):*

- GC • Carrying the board and rig to the water's edge and attaching them together in the water
- GC • Getting on the board, using uphaul for balance
- GC • Lifting the rig out of the water, establishing the secure position
- GC • Upwind rig recovery
- GC • Lowering the rig, coming ashore and positioning equipment safely
- GC • Boom height and adjustment

Sailing Techniques, Stance and Manoeuvres...

Can demonstrate:

- GC • Basic board-balancing exercises
- GC • Lying, kneeling and paddling the board either with or without a partner
- GC • Static steer, progressing on to turning through 180°, either nose or tail through the wind
- GC • Getting into the sailing position, sailing across the wind, turning the board and returning to shore
- GC • How to control the power in the rig
- GC • Stopping in control
- GC • Attracting attention
- GC • A basic method of self-rescue

SAILING BACKGROUND

Rigging

GC
Can assist with rigging the board

Rescue Techniques and Safety

Has an understanding of:

GC • Awareness of other water users

GC • The importance of self-help and self-rescue

GC • Alternative methods of rescue, their uses and limitations

GC • Attracting attention

Sailing Theory

GC • Can name basic components of the board and rig

GC • Has knowledge of the wind direction

Equipment

GC • Has knowledge and knows the importance of newcomers' boards and rigs (including size and suitability) and wearing a wetsuit and buoyancy aid

OTHER ASPECTS AND OPTIONS

• The Youth Stage 2 course

• Regular activity (clubs/Team15)

• An introduction to the racing syllabus and the Start Racing certificate

• Freestyle as a way to build on your ability and opportunity to log your progress

By the end of this first course you should be able to launch your equipment in the water and sail the board, returning to the original point on the shore by sailing or combining a method of self-rescue.

Rigging sticks can be used as an introduction to sections of this stage. However, to sign the elements, a rig must be used.

TAKE A CHALLENGE

• Dragging a foot in the water while sailing

• Clapping while sailing

• Starting from the beach as a group: sail or paddle around a buoy and return to the beach and see who gets back first – perhaps even get into teams and make the challenge into a relay!

ALL SECTIONS COMPLETED

_GC_

Chief Instructor/Principal signature

Centre stamp

YOUTH
Stage 2

During your Youth Stage 2 course your instructor will teach you the knowledge and practical skills to get you sailing around, practising tacking and gybing, and enabling you to make progression towards and away from the wind. It is assumed that before taking this course you will have mastered the practical skills and background knowledge required for Youth Stage 1.

PRACTICAL

Launching, Starting and Landing...

Has practical understanding of (with assistance if required):

- Launching the board and rig together
- Returning to shore in control and removing the board and rig from the water
- Leaving the board and rig on the shore safely

Sailing Techniques, Stance and Manoeuvres...

Can:

- Sail the board across the wind, turning between two points

  Steering

  - Steer the board towards the wind
  - Steer the board away from the wind
  - Sail the board between two points making ground towards and away from the wind

  Upwind and Tacking

  - Sail upwind
  - Tack on the move to change direction

Downwind and Gybing

- Sail downwind
- Perform a basic non-planing carve gybe on the move

SAILING BACKGROUND

Rigging

Has practical understanding of:

- Basic rigging, de-rigging and storage requirements
- The names and the uses of the main parts of the board and rig
- Boom height and adjustment

Can:

- Tie a figure of eight knot
- Tie a round turn and two half-hitches
- Tie a reef knot

Rescue Techniques and Safety

Has an understanding of:

- Safety equipment and essential spares

Sailing Conditions

Has basic knowledge of:

- The effects of onshore, cross-shore and offshore winds on a sailing area
- Weather forecasts: sources and a basic interpretation, effect on sailing area
- Tide predictions: sources and a basic interpretation; effect on sailing area (if applicable)
- The Beaufort Scale
- Personal limitations

Sailing Theory

Understands:

- The points of sailing
- The 'no-go zone' and its effect on the means of sailing upwind
- Terms – windward/leeward, upwind/downwind, port/starboard

Has knowledge of:

- The rules of the road – power gives way to sail, port versus starboard, overtaking vessel and windward vessel

Equipment

Has knowledge of and understands the importance of:

- The range of suitable clothing and accessories
- Types of wetsuit

OTHER ASPECTS AND OPTIONS

- The Youth Stage 3 course
- Opportunities for regular practice
- T15 and/or club activity

By the end of this stage you should have had a basic introduction to the background knowledge of windsurfing, be able to combine it with the practical skills to sail around a course, practise tacking and gybing, make progress upwind and downwind, and understand when to tack and gybe.

A static turn downwind is acceptable should the conditions be challenging.

TAKE A CHALLENGE

- Try kneeling while sailing
- Rig 180s
- Starting and finishing from the beach, sail around a three-buoy, downwind-slalom course. If you are really up for a challenge, combine this with the challenge in Youth Stage 1 – start afloat between two buoys with a ten-second warning before the GO!

ALL SECTIONS COMPLETED

Chief Instructor/Principal signature

Centre stamp

YOUTH
Stage 3

Once you have mastered the practical skills and knowledge required in Youth Stage 2, it's time to hook in and hang on! During this stage your instructor will help you to set up your board and rig correctly, enhance your stance on all points of sailing and introduce basic harnessing techniques in stronger winds.

PRACTICAL

Has developed an understanding of and can apply the Fastfwd Formula (Vision, Trim, Balance, Power and Stance) to:

Launching, Starting and Landing

Can:

- Carry and launch the board and rig together (alone or in pairs)
- Come ashore under control and land in stronger winds
- Remove the board and rig from the water, leaving them securely ashore

Beachstarting

Can:

- Recover the rig
- Control the board and rig together in the shallows
- Get onto the board in shallow water and sail away using a beachstart
- Beachstart in a variety of wind directions

Sailing Techniques, Stance and Manoeuvres

Can demonstrate the basic principles of the following:

- Improved stance on all points of sailing
- Gust control
- Altering the daggerboard to suit conditions and points of sailing
- Maintaining sailing line
- Improved steering using body weight and the rig
- Correct sail adjustment on all points of sailing

Harness

- Has a basic understanding of using the harness to improve trim, balance, power and stance
- Understands basic harness techniques
- Can adjust harness correctly
- Can hook in and out

Tacking

- Can maintain speed and flowing movement in stronger winds
- Has better use of the rig and weight control during:
  - Preparation and approach
  - Initiation

Gybing

- Can maintain speed and flowing movement in stronger winds
- Can develop body position throughout the non-planing carve gybe (NPCG)
- Has better use of the rig and weight control during:
  - Preparation and approach
  - Initiation
  - Rig rotation, timing and foot change
- Has improved the NPCG and downwind sailing, sailing clew first and steering on a run
- Has completed the NPCG using correct weight distribution in a variety of conditions, maintaining speed and power

SAILING BACKGROUND

Rigging

Can demonstrate the basic principles of the following:

- Choosing, rigging and de-rigging a sail suitable for the prevailing conditions
- Basic sail tuning
- Harness lines, correct positioning and adjustment

Rescue Techniques and Safety

Has understanding of:

- The importance of self-help and self-rescue
- Safety equipment and essential spares
- The importance of awareness of other water users

Sailing Conditions

Has basic knowledge of:

- Sea state in relation to the wind and tide
- Spotting deteriorating weather from visual sky signs
- Tides – springs/neaps, tidal streams, strength and visual signs
- Choosing a safe sailing location

SAILING THEORY

Has understanding of:

- The rules of the road – power gives way to sail, port versus starboard, overtaking vessel and windward vessel
- Wind awareness and its effect
- The parts of a board and rig
- The daggerboard and its effect; sailing with/without, on all points of sailing
- The Centre of Effort and Centre of Lateral Resistance and their effect
- The 'no-go zone' and its effect on sailing upwind

Equipment
Understands the importance of:

- Board types, uses and limitations
- The relationship between board volume and body weight
- Suitable clothing, accessories and seasonal suitability
- The advantages and disadvantages of different types of windsurfing equipment
- Board volume in relation to wind strengths, uses and limitations
- The types of harness and harness lines available
- Equipment – purchase, transport, storage and maintenance

OTHER ASPECTS AND OPTIONS

- The Youth Stage 4 course
- Becoming an assistant instructor and volunteering at your local club or training centre
- Different windsurfing pathways, and equipment options in relation to each

Having completed Youth Stage 3 you should be able to (with assistance) correctly set up your board and rig to the conditions, sail on all points, and understand when to tack and gybe, with and without the daggerboard (while understanding its uses and limitations).

You should also have a basic understanding of applying the Fastfwd Formula to aspects of your sailing and, by using an effective stance, show basic harnessing techniques. The skills and knowledge gained should mean you can now sail safely and in control.

TAKE A CHALLENGE

- Clew-first sailing
- Body 360s
- Sailing around a triangle without the daggerboard
- Ask your instructor to lay a course in the shape of a triangle starting from the beach. See who can sail around and back first. Make it really exciting and have a start line between a boat and a buoy or two, counting down for a start.

ALL SECTIONS COMPLETED

Chief Instructor/Principal signature

Centre stamp

YOUTH
Stage 4

Blasting around and getting in the footstraps is what this next stage is all about! On completing Youth Stage 4 you should have the confidence and ability to tack, gybe and sail in your harness with basic footstrap technique.

Successfully completing this course is the natural entry point into the Advanced course and clinics. It is assumed that before taking this course you will have mastered the practical skills and background knowledge required for the Youth Stage 3 course.

PRACTICAL

Has developed an understanding of, and can apply the Fastfwd Formula (Vision, Trim, Balance, Power and Stance) to:

Launching, Starting and Landing

Can:

- Carry and launch the board and rig together
- Use improved uphauling in planing conditions
- Stop under control
- Land and come ashore under control

Sailing Techniques, Stance and Manoeuvres

Can:

- Effectively use the board and sail to encourage planing
- Demonstrate improved harness technique and line adjustment for the conditions

- Effectively refine stance when hooked in, for the conditions, on all points of sail
- Cope with gusts and lulls

Footstraps

- Can correctly adjust the footstraps
- Understands basic footstrap technique
- Can make use of both footstraps
- Can maintain position in relation to the wind
- Can apply basic foot and toe pressure

Improved steering

- Can tack in stronger winds, maintaining speed into the turn and flowing movements
- Can perform the NPCG in stronger winds, maintaining speed and power, and demonstrate an ability to rotate the rig
- Can use daggerboard, sailing with/ without, on all points of sailing

SAILING BACKGROUND

Rigging

Can:

- Rig and de-rig
- Tune equipment to suit conditions
- Correctly adjust footstraps
- Tie a bowline

Rescue Techniques and Safety

Has an understanding of:

- Towing another board and sailor, tow lines and methods of attachments
- Actions to be taken in potential emergency situations
- Alternative methods of self-rescue

Sailing Conditions

Has an understanding of:

- Where to obtain a weather forecast
- Basic prediction of a synoptic chart
- Comparison with local conditions and expected changes
- Predicting changes in wind direction during a low-pressure system
- Wind and weather associated with a high-pressure system
- Using a tide table to obtain the time of high and low water, predicting expected changes and fastest flow, recognising dangerous tidal areas

- The effects of spring and neap tides
- Choosing a safe sailing venue considering the above, weather forecast and tidal information

Sailing Theory

Understands basic theory of:

- Apparent wind and its effect on the sail as speed changes
- Sailing upwind without a daggerboard
- How a sail works
- Fins and their effects on performance

Equipment

Has an understanding of:

- The advantages and disadvantages of different types of windsurfing equipment
- Lower volume boards, their uses and limitations
- Board volume in relation to wind strengths
- The types of harness and harness lines available
- Equipment care and storage
- Equipment: purchase, transport, storage and maintenance

ALL SECTIONS COMPLETED

Chief Instructor/Principal
signature

Centre stamp

OTHER ASPECTS AND OPTIONS

- The Advanced course and clinics
- Becoming a Start Windsurfing Instructor

Having completed Youth Stage 4 you should be able to set up your equipment correctly for the conditions, enabling you to show a confident ability to tack and gybe, sail in your harness and display basic footstrap technique. Youth Stage 4 is also the natural entry point for the Advanced courses.

TAKE A CHALLENGE

- Clew-first beachstarts
- Helicopter tack
- This will make you dizzy... Ask your instructor to lay a course with some buoys, setting a challenge to complete a certain number of tacks or gybes on the upwind and downwind legs. Adding a start line, with a countdown of two minutes, one minute, GO, will increase the challenge!

Advanced Windsurfing

On completion of the Advanced course you will be confident sailing in a variety of wind conditions and a range of equipment. Advanced coaching will increase your confidence in all conditions while providing you with improved blasting, tacking control and carving skills on varied water states.

Achieving all the skills and knowledge at the Advanced level may take extended coaching and practice time.

Throughout this level of the scheme, students should be introduced to the various clinics as well as elements such as freestyle to aid board and rig control.

It is assumed that any student on this course has mastered the practical skills and background knowledge required for the Youth Stage 4 course.

Advanced has a core section to be mastered, with two further clinics on waterstarting and carving skills.

PRACTICAL

Launching, Starting and Landing

Can:

- Perform controlled launching in a variety of conditions and water states
- Land and position equipment safely ashore
- Uphaul with refinements for lower-volume boards; uses and limitations

Has awareness of:

- Alternative carrying methods; considering board size, wind strength and direction

Sailing Techniques, Stance and Manoeuvres

Has developed an understanding of, and can apply the Fastfwd Formula (vision, trim, balance, power, stance) to:

- Get going
- Effectively use the board and sail to encourage early planing
- Achieve blasting control; maintain control in a variety of conditions including choppy water
- Refine stance according to conditions, on all points of sail; gusts and lulls
- Best use footstraps and harness

Can tack:

- In stronger winds using improved technique during entry, transition and exit
- Using differing volume boards suited to conditions

SAILING BACKGROUND

Rigging

Can:

- Rig and tune equipment to prevailing conditions

Rescue Techniques and Safety

Has knowledge of:

- Emergency repairs; action for broken fins, UJs and booms

Understands:

- Different methods of self-help, their uses and limitations
- How to help others in difficulty, with awareness of the situation and how to seek assistance

Sailing Conditions

Has an understanding of:

- The effects of high- and low-pressure systems on wind strength and direction
- Weather created by the passage of warm and cold fronts
- Tidal- and wave-driven effects: overfalls; races; rip currents; undertow; dumping waves – causes and effects
- Choosing a suitable sailing location: ideal conditions; tide/weather information

Sailing Theory

Has an understanding of:

- Spin out: causes; effects and solutions
- Leech twist

Equipment

Has an understanding of:

- Board design – rail shape; rocker; hull and tail shape; volume distribution
- Rigs – type; uses and limitations
- Fins – positioning; shape; design = performance
- Care and maintenance of equipment
- Latest developments in equipment

OTHER ASPECTS AND OPTIONS

- Advanced clinics
- Freestyle
- Racing pathways

ASSESSMENT CRITERIA

The students should be able to set up their board and rig suitably for their size and prevailing conditions. In various conditions and water states, students must be able to launch and recover their equipment; demonstrate an understanding of applying the Fastfwd Formula to tack efficiently; show effective stance on all points of sail; understand advanced getting going and blasting control techniques, and show an ability to sail safely and in control, with awareness of other water users, any hazards in their environment and knowledge of necessary actions to prevent rescue.

All criteria should be assessed on equipment suitable for the conditions.

ALL SECTIONS COMPLETED

Chief Instructor/Principal signature

Centre stamp

ADVANCED CLINICS

Waterstarting

The waterstart is introduced as a means of pulling yourself out of the water when you are at a stage where you wish to move on to lower-volume boards in open water.

Having completed the skills covered in the Advanced course, keep progressing and move on to the Advanced clinics. They are a natural progression and an amazing milestone in your windsurfing!

Pre-mastered fundamentals of the rig handling and power control used to complete the waterstart are a progressive link and development from those taught at beachstarting level. It is assumed that any student on this course has mastered the practical skills and background knowledge required for the Beachstart Clinic.

Has practical understanding and can:

- Set up board and rig correctly
- Control the board and rig together in deep water
- Show an understanding and awareness of hazards and keeping safe

Can:

- Complete the waterstart
- Vary technique for light and strong winds

ASSESSMENT CRITERIA

The students should be able to set up their board and rig correctly and suitably for their size and prevailing conditions, enabling them to sail at either a tidal or non-tidal location.

The assessment can be completed at either a tidal or non-tidal location, in conditions in which the students can comfortably plane.

Equipment used should be suitable for the prevailing conditions, with students showing an ability to sail safely and in control, with awareness of hazards in their environment and knowledge of necessary actions to prevent rescue.

ALL SECTIONS COMPLETED

Chief Instructor/Principal
signature

Centre stamp

Planing Carve Gybe

This is the skill every windsurfer throughout their progression aspires to – 'going round corners fast with style'.

Having practised and developed the core skills taught in the Advanced course, and the non-planing carve gybe, your instructor will expand and direct your knowledge towards the end goal of a fluid, controlled turn. During the course you will break down the fundamentals, approaching each section step by step.

On completion of this clinic you should be able to use the speed of the board combined with dynamic weight transfer to corner successfully with power and grace.

It is assumed that any student on this course has mastered the practical skills and background knowledge required for the Advanced Course and non-planing carve gybe.

PRACTICAL

Sailing Technique

Understands the principles of:

- Preparation
- Approach
- Initiation
- Body position
- Rig rotating, timing and foot change
- Maintaining speed and power through the turn
- Variations in technique to suit conditions

Can:

- Select and correctly tune equipment to conditions
- Complete the non-planing carve gybe
- Complete the planing carve gybe

ASSESSMENT CRITERIA

The assessment for the planing carve gybe may need to be carried out over a period of time at either an inland or coastal location, addressing the individual aspects that make up the manoeuvre.

The conditions and equipment used should enable the students to plane comfortably.

The students should also be able to set up their board and rig correctly and suitably for their size and prevailing conditions, enabling them to sail at either a tidal or non-tidal location, showing an ability to sail safely and in control, with awareness of hazards in their environment, showing knowledge of necessary actions to prevent rescue.

ALL SECTIONS COMPLETED

Chief Instructor/Principal signature

Centre stamp

RACING SYLLABUS

Start Racing

PRE-RACE PREPARATION

Equipment Preparation

Has an understanding of:

- Boom height
- How to prevent boom slippage
- Tightening battens
- Setting a sail for the conditions

Board and Kit Care

Can:

- Carry out a visual inspection, (looking for cracks, holes)
- Avoid damage, stones and rough surfaces

Health and Nutrition

Has knowledge of:

- Food as a fuel
- Keeping hydrated

Fitness

Has knowledge of:

- The physical demands of racing
- Performing basic injury prevention, i.e. warm up, cool down, stretching

TECHNIQUE

Starting

Can demonstrate the basics of:

- Getting near the start line on the gun
- Stopping and holding position

Speed

Can demonstrate the basics of:

- Developing stance
- Trimming the board upwind and downwind

Can demonstrate the basics of:

- Fluid tacks and gybes
- Gybing around a mark, entering wide and exiting tight

Can demonstrate the basics of:

- Keeping clear wind
- Tacking in the correct place for windward marks

RACING BACKGROUND

Racing Pathways and Structure

Has knowledge of:

- Team15 interclub challenges
- Scheme structure
- Equipment used in the RYA system

RACING THEORY

Racing Knowledge

Has an understanding of:

- A racing start line
- The port/starboard rule
- A simple starting sequence
- Being close to the start line on the gun
- Wind shadows
- The legs of a course, i.e. beat, reach, run

Wind/Weather/Tide

Can:

- Obtain and understand a simple weather forecast
- Select the correct rig and equipment for the conditions
- Understand high and low tide

Once you have completed Start Racing you should be able to race around a course in a small fleet and understand the starting procedure and course configuration.

TAKE A CHALLENGE

- Take part in an interclub event

ALL SECTIONS COMPLETED

Race Coach/Chief Instructor/
Principal signature

Centre stamp

Intermediate Racing

PRE-RACE PREPARATION

Equipment Preparation

Has an understanding of:

- Rig settings for different conditions
- Selecting the correct settings for the conditions
- Knowing when to change up or down a sail size
- Adjustable harness lines and setting the lines in the correct position
- Legal sail numbers and positioning

Board and Kit Care

Can:

- Ensure daggerboard works easily and effectively
- Keep fin and daggerboard in good condition

Health and Nutrition

Has an understanding of:

- Using food to enhance performance
- The effects of dehydration

Fitness

Has knowledge of:

- The requirement for physical fitness and training for racing
- Regular use of injury prevention techniques, warm up/cool down and stretching

TECHNIQUE

Starting

Can demonstrate the basics of:

- Reversing
- Controlling the board in tight situations
- Manoeuvring under control

Speed

Can demonstrate the basics of:

- Achieving the correct pointing angle
- Using railing upwind
- Rapid and efficient daggerboard movement relative to the leg of the course
- Correct use of the harness
- Pumping technique

Turning Techniques

Can demonstrate the basics of:

- Faster gybing in stronger winds
- Accelerating out of tacks and resuming pointing angle

Tactics and Strategy

Has knowledge and understanding of:

- Leeward mark roundings
- Deciding which side of the beat to go up and an awareness that the two sides may not be equal
- Spotting and using wind shifts on the upwind leg
- How to spot and react to gusts

RACING BACKGROUND

Racing Pathways and Structure

Has knowledge of:

- RYA Squad structures
- The equipment used in international Youth & Junior systems
- UKWA regional racing
- The role of the RYA and UKWA

RACING THEORY

Racing Knowledge

Has an understanding of:

- Racing courses
- The windward/leeward rule
- A standard starting sequence including flags
- Being on the start line on the gun
- Taking penalties (360°)
- Hailing protest
- Clear air and positioning at the start

Wind/Weather/Tide

Can:

- Obtain, understand and use a weather forecast
- Understand tides and timings of high and low water

The knowledge and practical experience gained by completing the Intermediate Racing Certificate should enable you to race around a course and make race decisions based upon rules and strategy with an awareness of other competitors.

TAKE A CHALLENGE

- Attend the RYA Zone championships

ALL SECTIONS COMPLETED

Race Coach/Chief Instructor/
Principal signature

Centre stamp

Advanced Racing

PRE-RACE PREPARATION

Equipment Preparation

Has an understanding of:

- Rig settings using adjustable outhaul and downhaul
- How to set a sail for maximum performance in all conditions
- Essential spares for competition
- Ensuring equipment is class-legal and complies with current class rules

Board and Kit Care

Can:

- Maintain foils and hull in good condition
- Demonstrate knowledge of basic board repair

Health and Nutrition

Has an understanding of:

- The use of sports drinks
- The effective use of food as a performance enhancer

Fitness

Has knowledge of:

- Establishing a basic fitness regime for windsurfing
- Incorporating body-weight training into a fitness programme

TECHNIQUE

Starting

Can demonstrate the basics of:

- Developing a starting plan
- Creating gaps on the start line using board control
- Accelerating and predicting the gun to ensure speed at the start

Speed

Can demonstrate the basics of:

- Using a tuning partner to test speed and height upwind
- Keeping a constant and smooth angle upwind
- Mast track adjustment
- Solid pumping technique both up and downwind
- Effective stance and control downwind

Turning Techniques

Can demonstrate the basics of:

- Carve gybing
- Faster 360° penalty turns

Tactics and Strategy

Has knowledge and understanding of:

- Pre-race planning, checking the course and making a decision as to which way to go
- Recognising and being aware of wind shifts
- Bearing away in a gust downwind

RACING BACKGROUND

Racing Pathways and Structure

Has knowledge of:

- UK racing structure/class associations and equipment
- Class rules
- National racing
- The role of qualification routes for RYA Zone/National squads

RACING THEORY

Racing Knowledge

Has an understanding of:

- The use of racing courses
- The basics of the Racing Rules of Sailing (RRS) part 1
- The basics of RRS part 2

Wind/Weather/Tide

Can:

- Understand and show awareness of the sea-breeze effect
- Predict conditions from simple weather forecasts
- Demonstrate an awareness of the relevance and effect of tidal streams

An Advanced Racing certificate means you have the skills to prepare yourself and race around a course in a large fleet and make decisions, using rules, tactics and strategy, both in regards to your own sailing and that of the fleet.

TAKE A CHALLENGE

- Enter the RYA Youth & Master Championships

ALL SECTIONS COMPLETED

Race Coach/Chief Instructor/
Principal signature

Centre stamp

Try something different

We have selected 10 freestyle skills for you to have fun with!

Having fun and trying new skills on your board is an essential way to help you progress in your windsurfing and on to more advanced skills.

They get slightly more advanced as you move from first to last. Try each move in light winds first and, as you get better, perhaps start trying them in a little more wind!

Sailing 'front to sail' builds on your ability to balance on the board, increases wind awareness and forms the foundations for other moves such as helicopter tacks, upwind and downwind 360s, and even spocks!

Perhaps make some moves up yourself or with friends and let us know how they are helping you progress and have fun with your windsurfing.

THE 10 FREESTYLE SKILLS...

1 **Lifting a foot/dragging a foot in the water**

   - Great for progressing on to beachstarts, waterstarts and general control of board, rig and yourself!

2 **Kneeling/sitting/lying down while sailing**

   - Good practice exercise for beachstarting and waterstarting

   - Enhances rig control by holding the foot of sail and mast only!

   - Gets a person moving on the board rather than being 'stuck' to it

3 **Switch-stance sailing**

   - Ties in with more advanced moves like duck tacks, push tacks and 'sliding' manoeuvres

4 **Clapping/pirouettes**

   - Teaches nature of rig balance and helps with 'ducking' of rig

   - Emphasises the use of your head and being nimble on your feet

5 **Rig 180s/rig 360s (ducking the rig)**

   - Gives great rig confidence and is vital for a high level of rig control

   - Great for progressing onto duck gybe and clew-first sailing

6 **Clew-first sailing/clew-first beachstarts**

   - Great for gybe exits (non-planing and planing)

   - Another vital skill to help give a high level of rig control

   - Helps progression for advanced skills such as grubbies

7 **Sailing backwards/sailing on the nose**

   - Helps with rig and board control

   - Helps progression on to willyskippers and stylish launching/landing at an awkward location!

8 **Body and rig 360**

   - Introduces concept of 'front to sail' and is great for nimble footwork!

   - Good building blocks for upwind 360s, backwind gybes, monkey and reverse monkey gybes

9 **Sailing 'front to sail'**

   - Gives a greater understanding of rig control

   - A pinnacle manoeuvre leading to better tacks, helicopter tacks, upwind 360s, tack and gybe variations

10 **Helicopter tack**

   - Try clew-first or switch-stance (or both!) variations

   - Combines a lot of the previous moves and skills

What's next?

ONBOARD

OnBoard (OB), the RYA's grassroots programme which started over 10 years ago with a set of ambitious targets, has reached some exceptional milestones. Reaching over half a million first-experience sailing and windsurfing sessions and over 50,000 regular sailors, the scheme continues to grow.

OnBoard gets you out on the water, teaches you new skills and lets you have great fun too!

Working with clubs and Recognised Training Centres across the UK, OB makes getting into sailing and windsurfing easy.

www.rya.org.uk/go/onboard

FANCY A GO AT RACING?

With a network of T15 clubs and local events to help introduce you to how much fun racing is, you may want to take one step further to progress and achieve your true potential. Open training sessions are organised locally, provided by expert coaches and delivered at clubs across the country.

You may also want to consider attending your local RYA Zone or Home Country Championship – these usually take place on the last weekend in September each year and enable young sailors to show off their skills under the watchful eye of RYA High Performance Managers and Coaches.

Following this training, you can apply for the RYA Zone Squad depending on your age and ability. Zone Squads are designed to feed talented sailors into the RYA National Junior Squad programme, enabling them to develop and ultimately succeed at various championships. For more information and details, check out the National Junior Squad section of the RYA website (www.rya.org.uk) or contact the RYA Racing Department directly.

TEAM15

Team15 (T15) is a nationwide network of clubs where the coolest windsurfers aged 16 or under get together every week, learn new skills and have a great time.

Team15 clubs operate at recognised RYA Windsurfing Centres. Getting into the T15 clubbin' scene is easy, it doesn't cost the earth and, if you're just starting out, we even provide all the equipment. Whether you windsurf already or are just taking your first go, T15 is the place to be.

Once you are totally hooked, you'll want to aim to get into your T15 club team, a specially selected team of 15 who represent their club at four annual inter-club events. For further information check it out online: www.team15.org.uk.

THE DUKE OF EDINBURGH'S AWARD

Are you aged between 14 to 24 and fancy challenging yourself?

The RYA is recognised as a National Operating Authority for The Duke of Edinburgh's Award (DofE). The DofE is a voluntary, non-competitive programme of activities for anyone aged 14 to 24, providing a fantastic opportunity to experience new activities or develop existing skills.

There are three progressive levels of programmes that, when successfully completed, lead to a Bronze, Silver or Gold Award.

SAILING AS PART OF YOUR DofE

Achieving a DofE Award can be made an adventure from beginning to end. Within an RYA club or training centre there are already many activities you could take part in that can count towards your DofE. These could range from:

Volunteering: Helping out at your local training centre, club or Team15 night on a regular basis. This could be as an assistant, in the kitchen or maybe even on the committee!

Physical: Are you regularly taking part in sailing or windsurfing activity such as Team15? Why not set yourself a goal to gain a certain certificate in the RYA National Sailing or Windsurfing scheme, or maybe participate in regular club racing?

Skill: All about developing your skills, whether practical, social or personal. You may choose to sharpen up your powerboating, learn a new skill such as boat repair work, become an instructor or perhaps increase your theory knowledge and learn all about meteorology!

Residential and Expedition: You may never have been away from home before, let alone used your board or boat to go on an exciting adventure with friends, so now is the time!

Further information can be found, explaining the opportunities available, on the DofE website www.dofe.org, and the RYA website www.rya.org.uk/go/dofe.

BECOMING AN INSTRUCTOR – INSTRUCTOR PATHWAY

With windsurfing having grabbed your attention you may wish to pass the skills you have learnt from this infectious sport to others. You can start your progression on the instructional ladder once you have achieved your Youth Stage 3 certificate. You could then become an Assistant Instructor at your local training centre.

Upon turning 16, you may choose to become a fully qualified RYA Start Windsurfing Instructor. Full details on becoming an instructor are available on the RYA website (www.rya.org.uk).

INTRODUCING RACING INTO YOUR CENTRE OR CLUB

f you have basic racing experience or would like to be given the opportunity to learn basic race-coaching techniques, the Racing Instructor course will cover instructional techniques afloat and ashore. Candidates do need to be a minimum of a Start Windsurfing Instructor to attend this course or gain this qualification.

Race Coaching Pathway

Playing a part in helping develop talented windsurfers to progress and achieve their goals in our fantastic sport is a great feeling. The RYA race coach schemes allow individuals with knowledge and experience the chance to gain skills in order to progress in the world of coaching. Coaches play a massive role in the RYA programmes, from regional and junior up to Olympic level, and if you feel that this is a route that you would like to pursue, full details are available on the RYA website (www.rya.org.uk).

Personal Log

Date...	Location...	Board...	Rig...	Conditions...	Activity...
AUG 2016	RWS	BIC BEACH	7.5.	F 3	STAGE 1

Personal Log

Date...	Location...	Board...	Rig...	Conditions...	Activity...

Personal Log

Date...	Location...	Board...	Rig...	Conditions...	Activity...

Personal Log

Date...	Location...	Board...	Rig...	Conditions...	Activity...

Personal Log

Date...	Location...	Board...	Rig...	Conditions...	Activity...

Personal Log

Date...	Location...	Board...	Rig...	Conditions...	Activity...

Congratulations on achieving your first windsurfing certificate

YOUTH
Stage 1

Please attach your RYA certificate here

Please note that no record of certificates is held by the RYA

Enquiries about lost certificates should be made to the centre where the course was taken

YOUTH
Stage 2

Please attach your RYA certificate here

Please note that no record of certificates is held by the RYA

Enquiries about lost certificates should be made to the
centre where the course was taken

YOUTH
Stage 3

Please attach your RYA certificate here

Please note that no record of certificates is held by the RYA

Enquiries about lost certificates should be made to the
centre where the course was taken

YOUTH
Stage 4

Please attach your RYA certificate here

Please note that no record of certificates is held by the RYA

Enquiries about lost certificates should be made to the
centre where the course was taken

Advanced Windsurfing

Please attach your RYA certificate here

Please note that no record of certificates is held by the RYA

Enquiries about lost certificates should be made to the centre where the course was taken

Racing Syllabus

Racing

Please attach your RYA certificate here

Please note that no record of certificates is held by the RYA

Enquiries about lost certificates should be made to the centre where the course was taken

Notes

Notes

Notes

w.rya.org.uk/go/join

OVE TO WINDSURF?

...en why not join the association that supports you?

Join the RYA today and benefit from

- ...ree third party insurance
- ...epresenting your interests and defending your rights of navigation
- ...ersonal advice and information on a wide range of windsurfing topics
- ...ree sail numbers for Gold Members
- ...egal advice on buying, selling and other windsurfing related matters
- ...he latest news delivered to your door or inbox by RYA magazine and e-newsletters
- ...oat show privileges including an exclusive free RYA members' lounge
- ...iscounts on a wide range of products and services

Get more from your boarding; support the RYA

...ant to know more?

...en call our friendly and helpful membership team on 0844 556 9556 or email: member.services@rya.org.uk

...ne RYA... be part of it   www.rya.org.uk